I0211065

VESTIGES

poems by

Savannah Grant

Finishing Line Press
Georgetown, Kentucky

VESTIGES

ACKNOWLEDGMENTS

"The Disruption II" and "...It Wasn't That" were published in *Sixfold Journal*
online, Issue No. 25, Winter 2024

Publisher: Leah Huete de Maines
Editor: Christen Kincaid
Cover Art: Savannah Grant
Author Photo: Savannah Grant
Cover Design: Elizabeth Maines McCleavy

Order online: www.finishinglinepress.com
also available on amazon.com

Author inquiries and mail orders:
Finishing Line Press
PO Box 1626
Georgetown, Kentucky 40324
USA

Contents

For Juniper

The Disruption II

They are dredging the pond

the new brown landscape only
half a shock
not frightening
dug-up leaves crumpled around each other in dirt
body sized

this is something I've seen or only
half seen
tried to talk to as if what happened didn't matter
to us
        the leaves and me

we've entered November heavily
with the strength I need to be
here

listen
I need to tell you something about sitting at that table
with stringy hair after a shower
shoving pills down a cat's throat
        rotting alive
because we cannot talk to each other
as if I've never been unrecognizable

        they are dredging the pond

the trees there are silent, they know
sometimes ponds need to be dredged
the edges of the water have iced and the same geese as last year
leave again
to come back in April

Knives

We both like knives
that was one reason why
         to you I was perfect

the burden of perfect
         keeps my door shut

I never use my knife for anything
but I threw yours into the floor one night
a black snap-shut sharp steel

you must have loved that I loved it
watched like a panther you
fling it point-down through the rug
into whatever moldy floor was beneath

         I flung it next

laughed at the thud and it stood up
point-first in the middle
of the small dingy room with the
broken things all inside of it

September

Strange how my death hangs behind me
like an overweight pear

when I pulled leaves instead of
that root
and now the trees with male-pattern baldness

      show every wasp nest
      and fall fruits I am indifferent to

that root holds fast and rice paper
skin held next to ribs cries out
for new seams

In Which I Try to Find the Quarry Without You

By the way, I could not
      I don't think
      I'm supposed to

the air full of sweetfern

there are no lessons to be learned from you
except that I should not have
let it go

         wildfire sky in September
         and if it has reached us

the least I can do is give back
some of the bravery
you gave me

Late Fall Walk

1

They were dark thin days
splinters etched in metal
and printed again and again so everyone could see it
while I tried to forget certain things

everyone on the sidewalk
and in the hallway was you
so I pinched my arms
to leave tiny scars

stayed awake
in the heaviness of not quite rain
stamping on puffball mushrooms in brown boots with you

there are places I no longer walk

I listened to loud music to escape you
next to me
while I lied
beside the river and wet woods
scrambled down a wall of chicken wire and rocks
through the gate where an exuberant dog
got us muddy

I said I was okay
just tired

2

I separate the times you were here
according to weather and dark
once the air was too heavy to move
but we walked for hours

the Halloween air opaque with snow

the power went out and we sat in my doorway while the
leftover light
in my room rotted

you slept in my bed twice
and my shaking pooled too heavy
to send out the window
so I gagged in the basement among mirror shards

took pictures of the dark through windows
to understand what I was afraid of

and when you left the whole town was dark under snow
I couldn't stop walking in circles
tried to eat bread
on the floor in the only corner left
without rotten light

3

I thought I was supposed to endure
the dim light from the hallway
as if that's what love was

the morning after
on the balcony in October
under too much snow

Drain

I turned sour that night

perhaps
anxiety hunger almost sex

together a tremor I
thought I was done with
spilled out wanting

leaked
a different smell to my legs
spread and stuck
woke up with it

I could never sleep
with someone else touching me
yet shifted fingers across your collar bone
that was as far
as I could go

I listened
made sure your heart sped up

you said I shiver in my sleep
I was awake and cold
draining

The Nature of This Pain

Perhaps the nature of this pain
is dull

I have trouble remembering faces and voices
just a chipped front tooth
and two silver molars
in my room turned dark grey

I checked
your eyes were dark green
I wish I didn't know what it looked like
when I couldn't do it for you

this distance from you is an act
on the edge of my bed
you make no sense

as I return to myself
stung by nettles on a humid June afternoon
along a narrow trail we walk single file

Try

You were wrong about me in the way
that you were wrong about how often it rains

how long it takes to realize me
in the way you don't recognize your room
when you first wake up

I've been asking
and asking for rivers in July
eyes like that
just you as you are

but I got brown leather oxfords with an obvious
heel scuff
what did you expect in a fancy shirt like that
all these uphill walks with me

House Cleaner's Prayer

What the government doesn't know about what happens
when I enter rooms
I make them better

I am as America is
on my knees in dust
scrubbing someone else's coffee stains

I rise to un-cobweb your ceilings

what I see in this stark hallway

what I find in empty houses
what I bring and what I leave behind

what I clear away and what I make room for

isn't pennies
or toast crumbs

Wrong Line Blues

I peel the brussels sprouts I bought
trying to get in his checkout line at the store
and think about how I've been changed
the one thing I didn't want to believe

I hear there is still more I must do

but I don't understand why it is so hard to talk to someone
who smiled at me once months ago
so I forget something on purpose
trying to get in his line at the store again

I Stooped Low Again Today

I stooped low again today

asked a louder question
I already knew the answer
just not why
the answer was that

after, I went upstairs
folded laundry
sweating on my nice rug and
playing music

amazing
I still do this when you're
all out of reach

Tragedy Clothes

I keep a list of what I call
tragedy clothes
a list of things I remember and then miss
and sometimes I type in
polka-dot-tube-top or lilac-suede-boots
just to see
if they're still for sale online somewhere

because when I wore them I was alive
and for some reason
didn't want them anymore

After, You Give Up

I am a ghost in these houses I clean
that's how I want it to be and

I don't want to go
where I know I have to go without you

heel scuff
        damaged
you'll find any walk with me sickening

Skin Hunger

Meet me at the river in July

beneath fireworks

half-asleep, my head buzzing
against your shoulder

Vignette, 1:17am

You're in your roommate's car during pandemic
and you don't particularly
even like him
but he drove you to the vet because
your cat was screaming from under the dresser
and your car wouldn't start

and your mouth is dry

and he's looking at the stars
through his phone

and the spring peepers are out

You Don't Understand Poetry

But on your hand a white ink monarch
and you won't tell me which day in July

and now you make scrambled eggs the way I told you

I don't listen as you talk about White Mountains from my one
rickety kitchen chair because one eye green and the other brown

       thinking your shoulders are mine
       your fingers are mine

how can you stand a metal railing in winter so I put my mittens
under your hands
       how I wanted you to mean what I wanted you to mean

I wished you hadn't shifted me above you when I just wanted my
arm over your neck

       your hair in the mornings like oceans

how like words I dreamed
but could never get down I thought you could have been perfect

Sunday in March

My feet go numb in a big red truck
blue-eyed
a loud Irishman

nothing like you
today I don't want silence
and for too long I sat
in new-car smell

you and I fit
in my one rickety kitchen chair
me holding onto you like I try to make meaning
in your loss

I know what of myself
I keep hidden this time
rivulets in rain

the patterns I see there
but this is just a date
four hours talking in a truck
will not make me forget you

September II

The leaf smell haunts me like
a death inside myself I didn't plan for
our love is not a house
my love looks out to sea

with the music of a wedding behind me
I try to hear instead the wind in the wet air
because you do not come back when I open the door
to let you in

like a lighthouse maybe
out there in the fog

I always end up by water
          waiting at your shore

Gratitude

Only two years ago on the coldest night I opened the window
to see how long I could stand it
practicing
and in this room here two nights ago
after you left I wanted to tell you about it

if anyone

brown eyes
Alaska
you had me
shaking

laughing when you scrawled

Depression!

across a wet window
oh to love freely
            safely

The Day Before the Hunger Moon

Tall drink of water
slippery like watermelon seeds even in February
and all I want is to make it to summer with you

I do everything I can to settle it
knowing it will be wormy March until it's all been
       waited for
and we're not what we want
       intrinsically

or April or June
no one's told me what else I need to wait for
and I can't sleep with Mercury falling like this

I mean it this time
who could possibly be after you?

Vignette, 1:44am

A tail curled
tiny breath on my fingernail

I have nightmares about open doors

despite her furry twitching ears
it's cold thinking about

you
not knowing each other anymore

You Sat Next to Me and Wrote About Her

The caption is deleted but the picture
like a card trick hidden up your sleeve
still exists between the rest of them and I still remember it
as if it still exists between us

how painful it is
that you took pictures of her at all
in the sand and by the window

almost as if you didn't want me to know
that you kept mistaking her
for me

When You Leave Again

When you leave again
in the arms of the woods I fall

lie there obliquely
with my carefulness
whisper things to you

is this the wrong way to love you?
you're the only thing
that makes me feel like I'm here

I set myself up for losing you
                    again

still learning how to live this way
knowing I'll

never be the one you take pictures of

back to wandering a parking garage at night
with a dead car battery

back to a blizzard that could have been
your couch

I Sweep the Floor

I sweep the floor like I do
almost every night
in an apartment not empty enough

your loss is the only one I can't find all the answers for

but we're too old to wave away our differences
they're under us
a riverbed

we could work through that snowstorm in 2017
driving home alone
ninety-three miles at night because you forgot

we could work through your pain
that started here
you'd sit on the same dock when she was too much in February

       it wasn't the pictures of her
       that hurt me

but in the mornings I pull open the blinds and make my bed
sweep the floors
look for you in the parking lot
I waited years

what matters is you'd never love like I do

I waited years only to talk to you
as if it didn't matter
unreconcilable that how much I love you won't ever be
enough

Body Apology

I will write my body an apology
because it will not let me lie to it again

while I wait for America to apologize to itself
its own fields
and wolves and cloud-shadows of bison
the heat of March

I will not wait to feed you or
make you afraid to bleed
and think you are going back to that colorless place
that hungry place

I don't have to wait for someone
to take the place of someone who keeps me awake at night
with lights and doors
like my mother did
or a boy from election night four years ago
as if this afternoon I have to wait
as if I don't deserve fresh grapes or
maple syrup

...It Wasn't That

I thought going under for twenty minutes
a dose of Propofol
would make the years without myself irrelevant
      a diagnosis

so I wouldn't have to have been in that parking garage elevator
with two strange men
or my sickness would have been damage
only intestinal
I wouldn't have to have been glassy-eyed
in a car with someone I'd never love

could this be the answer to end all the answers I wanted?
it's fine
      it started at birth
you got this from your mother
genetic depression
      from too much bread

I would drive away from the hospital
      peace
after a physician came up with *Celiac*

      what then of revelation? what then
      of screaming and purging the weight of it all?

years of losing my brain to laminate floors
and gritty carpet and the corners of my lips
to a bathroom mirror wondering
who
      this
            was
could be *Celiac*

with one appointment I could turn the reason I needed to
die into *Celiac*—my god

    on the water
    speaks to me and says I will not be made irrelevant
    I am more than villi
    more than atrophy
    I will not be seen that way
    with a camera
    down your throat

Song to Myself

I promise being loved is not a miracle
it is not rare:

it is sparrows in the dust
it is that one sunset over a strip mall parking lot
it is leaves turning their pale underbellies to the sky
before a summer storm

that same rain falls on your face and we love you
the sun rises again tomorrow and we love you
dragonflies zip along the river
and still we love you

I promise this is not the end

for it is your name I scream when I jump thirty feet into the water
and when I can breathe again the sun is all I see
blurred through the trees in June
clawing my way back onto the rocks

yes the fall is farther than I thought
and yes my shins are bruised
and yes it feels like my lungs collapsed—

I made myself this dam of iron and rocks
when I wanted to be willow and water
when my gentleness eroded
I wanted to be remade for you

we carry stars between us both in distance and in light
still we grow around each other like tree rings
I would ask you if time was the river or if time was the sand
either way I would keep your fingers entwined with mine

Savannah Grant is an artist and poet living in Western MA. She returned to the area in 2018 after attending Smith College and has been living there ever since. She was an English major and studio art minor with concentrations in poetry and intaglio printmaking. At Smith, her writing received prestigious awards for short stories and poetry collections.

Savannah's individual poems have been published in the online reader-voted journal *Sixfold* in 2014, 2018, 2023, and 2024. She has two additional chapbooks titled *at the end of gospel* and *Had I, I Would Have* available from Bottlecap Press, a small independent millennial-run press. She has more collections and individual poems in the works as well!

Savannah's paintings, digital art, etchings, and monotype prints have appeared in galleries throughout downtown Northampton and the greater Pioneer Valley area, most notably A.P.E. Gallery's Flat File 2022 and Microworks 2023 shows. She is an active member at Zea Mays Printmaking in Florence, MA and has prints available for sale in their flat file collection.

Savannah is a house cleaner by day and loves to attend local live music shows by night! When she is not working on new art or poems, she is out in nature, biking, cooking, or spending time with her community of friends. She has a lovely little cat named Juniper.